001

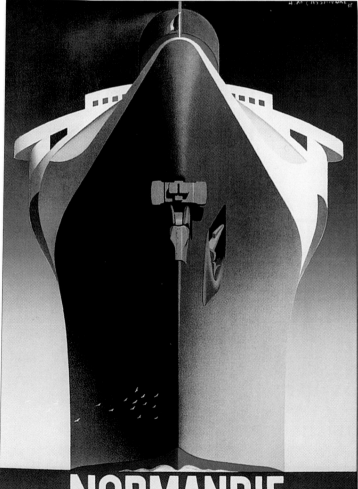

003

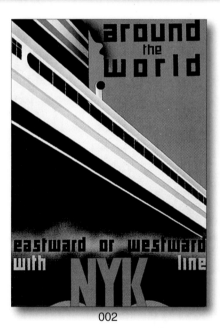

002

004

THE NEW s.s. *Independence* and s.s. *Constitution*

006

STUTTGART

008

005

United States Lines

S.S. Manhattan

007

2

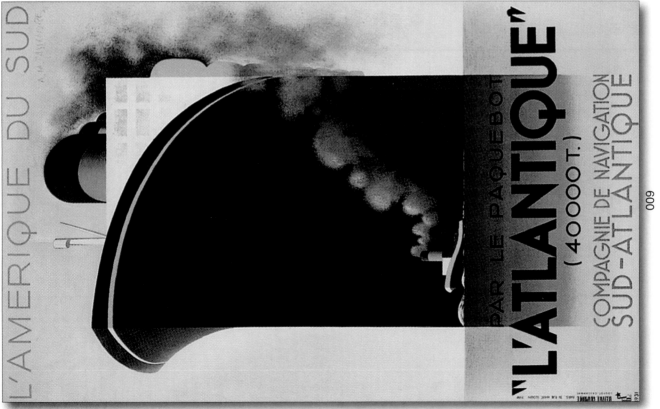

012

S.S. CONSTITUTION · AMERICAN EXPORT LINES

014

011

013

4

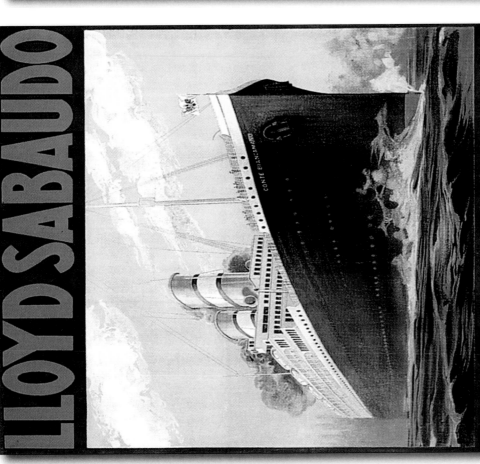

LLOYD SABAUDO

CONTE BIANCAMANO
CONTE ROSSO ★ CONTE VERDE
Servizi celeri di gran lusso per le Americhe

STAB. G. SCHENONE-GENOVA

015

NEW YORK
ANCHOR LINE
TO AND FROM
VIA MOVILLE (LONDONDERRY)
GLASGOW.

016

5

017

018

P. & O. S.S. VICEROY OF INDIA, 19,700 TONS GROSS.
India Mail and Passenger Service.

019

020

021

022

023

024

7

026

028

Cunard R.M.S. "Scythia"

025

027

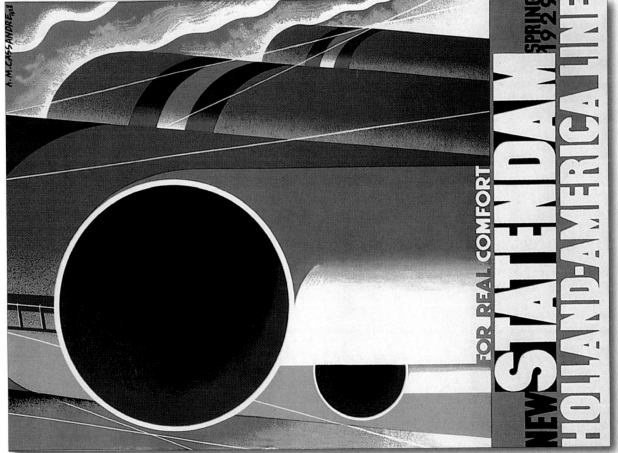

032

The Hamburg-American Line Piers, Hoboken, N. J.

034

S.S. "Merion."

031

033

10

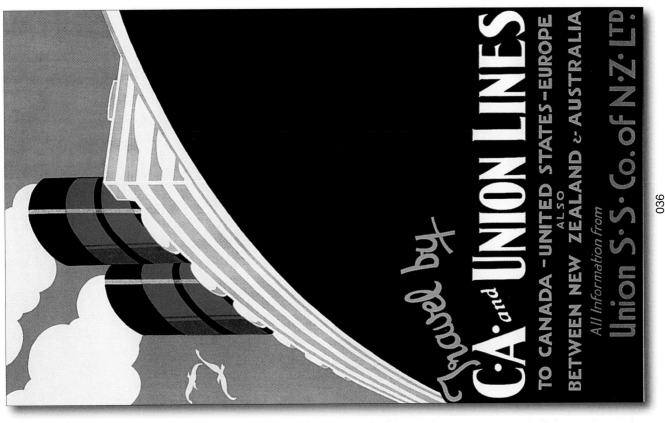

036

035

037

Cunard R.M.S. 'Parthia'

038

039

The Leviathan Leaving
New York City.

040

042

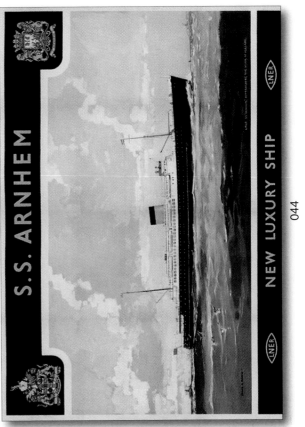

044

041

043

046

Cunard R.M.S. "Franconia"

048

WHITE STAR LINE
TRIPLE-SCREW S.S. "LAURENTIC."

045

ANCHOR LINE—T.S.S. CALEDONIA

047

050

049

15

CUNARD R.M.S. BERENGARIA TONNAGE 52,300

051

RED STAR
LINE.

TRIPLE-SCREW
"BELGENLAND"
27.200 TONS

052

S. S. Imperator, Hamburg American Line.
Largest in the World.
50,000 Tons—900 Feet Long.

053

054

055

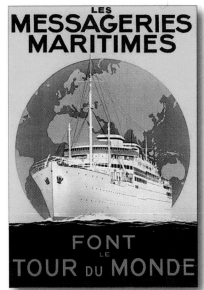

056

057

058

059

CIᴱ Gᴸᴱ TRANSATLANTIQUE · FRENCH LINE

"NORMANDIE" LE HAVRE · SOUTHAMPTON · NEW YORK

061

R. M. S. Queen Elizabeth

063

INMAN STEAMSHIP COMPANY.

060

062

Comfort-Courtesy-Safety-Speed
UNITED STATES LINES

065

SUÈDE
VIA LONDRES

Billets à bas prix de Paris
à toutes les Stations Suédoises

s.s. SUECIA
s.s. BRITANNIA
s.s. PATRICIA

SWEDISH LLOYD GOTHEMBOURG-SUÈDE

064

19

FURNESS PRINCE LINE

NEW YORK - SOUTH AMERICA SERVICE

067

069

SOUTHERN PACIFIC STEAMSHIP LINES (MORGAN LINE) S. S. DIXIE—NEW YORK—NEW ORLEANS

ACCLAIMED ONE OF THE STAUNCHEST VESSELS EVER TURNED OUT OF A SHIPYARD

066

S/S SUECIA — S/S BRITANNIA

068

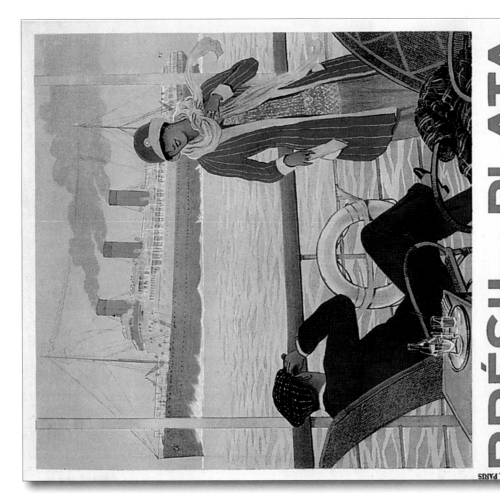

BRÉSIL - PLATA

PAR LES COMPAGNIES DE NAVIGATION

CHARGEURS RÉUNIS
SUD-ATLANTIQUE

071

N.R.MONEY, 6 Rue de Madrid, PARIS

Leviathan at Southampton

UNITED STATES LINES
Europe ~ America

070

21

Cunard R.M.S. "Mauretania"

073

The New "Mauretania"

Cunard White Star

075

AMERICAN PRESIDENT LINES'
S.S. PRESIDENT WILSON
CALIFORNIA TO THE ORIENT

072

CUNARDER AT SOUTHAMPTON.

074

CROISIERES ET CIRCUITS
"TRANSAT"
Cⁱᵉ Gⁱᵉ TRANSATLANTIQUE

076

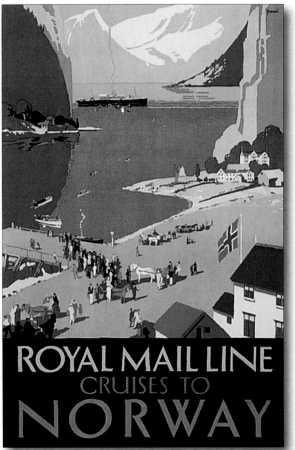

ROYAL MAIL LINE
CRUISES TO
NORWAY

077

CHEMINS DE FER DE PARIS LYON MÉDITERRANÉE

THONON LES BAINS
BILLETS DE STATIONS THERMALES À PRIX RÉDUITS. Hᵗᵉ SAVOIE

078

INDOCHINE
東
法

CHARGEURS
REUNIS

079

S.S. ORSOVA, ORIENT LINE

28,790 GROSS TONS.　LENGTH 690 FT.　BEAM 90 FT.　SPEED 26 KNOTS

080

081

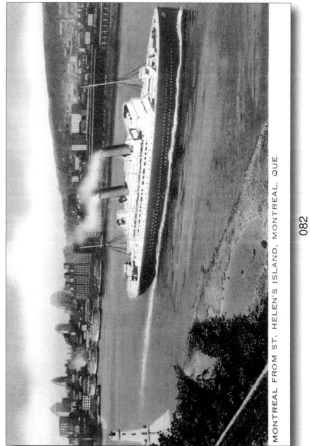

MONTREAL FROM ST. HELEN'S ISLAND. MONTREAL. QUE.

082

Osaka—Beppu Liner, M.S. "Sumire Maru" O.S.K. LINE　大阪商船別府航路　すみれ丸

083

24

085

084

25

087

HOLLAND–AMERICA LINE.

ROTTERDAM – NEW YORK

T.S.S. ROTTERDAM. 24170 TONS REGISTER - 37190 TONS DISPLACEMENT.

089

HOLLAND-AMERICA LINE.

ROTTERDAM - NEW YORK
VIA BOULOGNE-SUR-MER.

T.S.S. NIEUW-AMSTERDAM. 17250 Tons Register - 31000 Tons Displacement.

086

Cunard M.V. Britannic

088

090

091

093

092

094

S. S. Berengaria, Cunard Line, New York

096

LENGTH 500 FEET·BREADTH 98 FEET 6 INCHES·510 STATEROOMS·SPEED 22 MILES PER HOUR

"SEEANDBEE"

098

095

"Georgic"

Cunard White Star

097

28

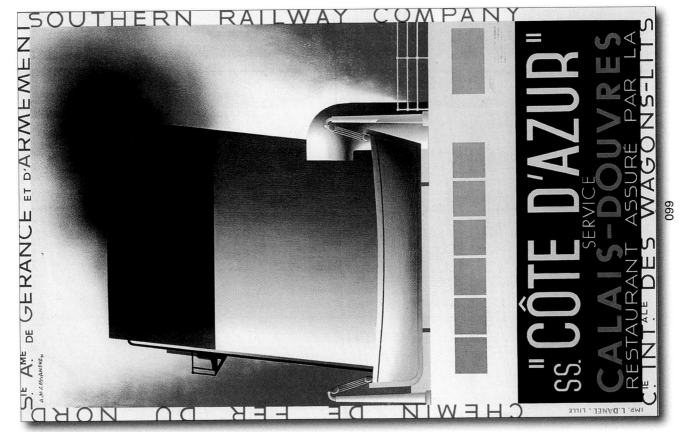

101

WHITE STAR LINE
TWIN-SCREW R.M.S. "HOMERIC."

102

CLYDE-MALLORY LINER APPROACHING JACKSONVILLE, FLA.

103

Swedish American Liner leaving New York

104

106

105

31

DONALDSON-ATLANTIC LINE—TURBINE TWIN-SCREW STEAMSHIP "LETITIA."

108

110

S.S. "CITY OF PARIS," 10,200 TONS.

107

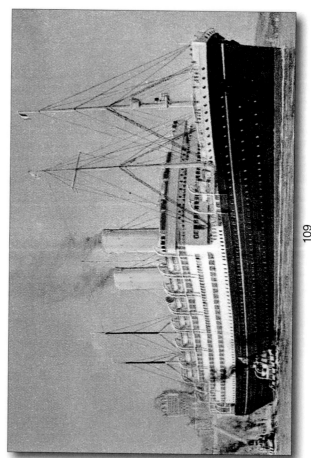

109

33

Hamburg-Amerika Linie

Doppelschrauben-Postdampfer „Amerika"

113

God guard thee from the dangers of the sea

114

HOLLAND-AMERICA LINE

NEW YORK - ROTTERDAM

DUTCH COSTUMES NOORD-HOLLAND.

115

WHITE STAR LINE

T.S.S. TITANIC.

116

117

118

119

120

121

122

HOLLAND-AMERICA LINE.　　ROTTERDAM-NEW YORK

T.S.S. STATENDAM. 30000 Tons Register - 40000 Tons Displacement.

124

The Cunard White Star Liner "Queen Mary."

126

R.M.S. Queen Mary

Cunard White Star

123

HOLLAND-AMERIKA LINIE.

ROTTERDAM-NEW YORK
ROTTERDAM-HALIFAX (KANADA) } DIREKT

D.D. VEENDAM. 15450 Register Tons - 25600 Tons Wasserverdrängung.

125

127

128

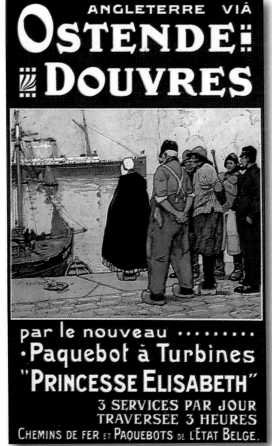

129

130

WHITE STAR LINE
TRIPLE-SCREW R.M.S. "OLYMPIC."

132

134

RED STAR LINE.

TRIPLE-SCREW "WESTERNLAND" 16.500 TONS.

131

133

136

135

WHITE STAR
LINE

TWIN-SCREW R.M.S. "CELTIC."
21,179 TONS.

138

THE NEW CUNARDER "ANDANIA" 14,000 TONS

140

WHITE STAR LINE

"CEDRIC" LEAVING LIVERPOOL

137

S. S. "ST. JOHN" ON EASTERN S. S. LINES, INC.

139

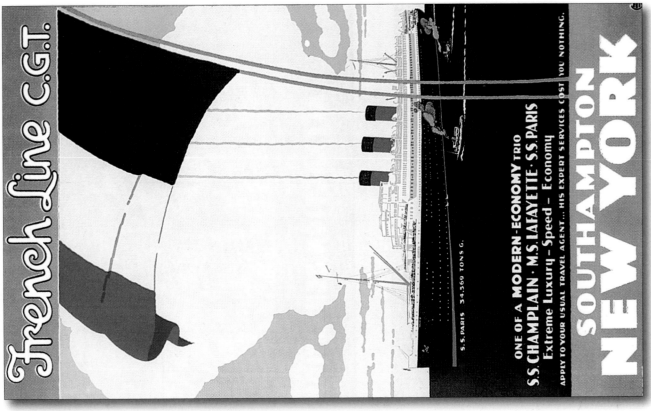

142

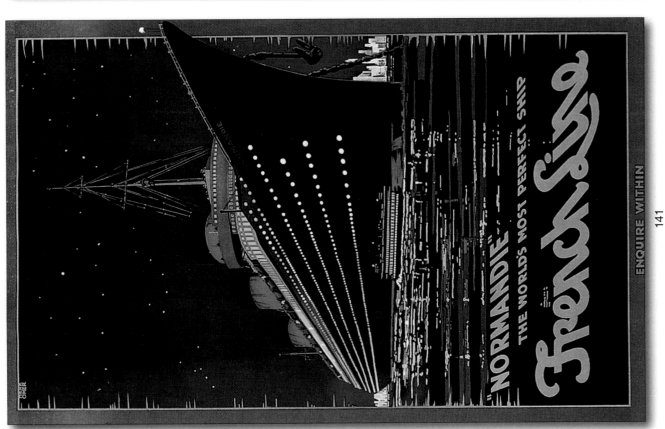

141

144

WHITE STAR LINE
TWIN-SCREW S.S. "DORIC."

146

PANAMA PACIFIC LINER IN PEDRO MIGUEL LOCKS, PANAMA CANAL

143

145

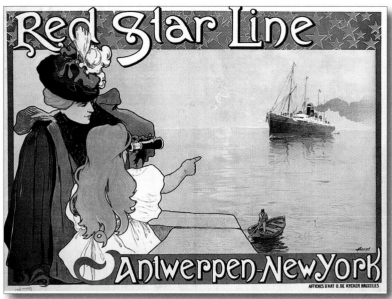

147

148

149

150

151

152

Hamburg-Amerika Linie

An Bord der „Amerika" den

154

P. & O. TWIN SCREW PASSENGER STEAMSHIP "CUBA"

341 FT. LONG, 47 FT. WIDE, SPEED 17 KNOTS PER HOUR, PASSENGER CAPACITY 520

156

M.V. "STAFFORDSHIRE."

BIBBY LINER

153

HOLLAND-AMERICA LINE.

ROTTERDAM—NEW YORK } DIRECT
ROTTERDAM—HALIFAX (CANADA) } SERVICE

T.S.S. VOLENDAM. 15430 TONS REGISTER – 25620 TONS DISPLACEMENT.

155

158

157

45

THE SS MARIPOSA, 632 FEET LONG; 79 FEET BREADTH; GROSS TONNAGE 19,000; SPEED 22½ KNOTS

160

162

159

President Lincoln.

161

163

The New White Star Liner,
R.M.S. "TITANIC"

provides for her first-class passengers
VINOLIA OTTO TOILET SOAP
the highest standard of Toilet Luxury and comfort at sea.

VINOLIA COMPANY LTD., LONDON AND PARIS.

164

47

166

"La Lorraine"

C.ⁱᵉ G.ᵗᵉ TRANSATLANTIQUE
(FRENCH LINE)

168

S.S."ILE DE FRANCE"
(COMPAGNIE GÉNÉRALE TRANSATLANTIQUE)
LEAVING HAVRE

165

167